SKOKIE PUBLIC LIBRARY

W9-AXK-928

MAR   2011

From China to America:
The Story of *Amy Tan*

From China to America:
The Story of *Amy Tan*

Greensboro, North Carolina

SKOKIE PUBLIC LIBRARY

WORLD WRITERS

ROBERT FROST

STEPHEN KING

JANE AUSTEN

CHARLES DICKENS

RALPH ELLISON

O'HENRY

ROALD DAHL

JONATHAN SWIFT

LEO TOLSTOY

ZORA NEALE HURSTON

MARK TWAIN

MARY SHELLEY

C.S. LEWIS

RALPH WALDO EMERSON

AMY TAN

World Writers

From China to America: The Story of Amy Tan

Copyright © 2011 by Morgan Reynolds Publishing

All rights reserved
This book, or parts therof, may not be reproduced
in any form except by written consent of the publisher.
For more information write:
Morgan Reynolds Publishing, Inc.
620 South Elm Street, Suite 387
Greensboro, NC 27406 USA

Library of Congress Cataloging-in-Publication Data

O'Keefe, Sherry.
From China to America : the story of Amy Tan / by Sherry O'Keefe. -- 1st ed.
p. cm. -- (World writers)
Includes bibliographical references and index.
ISBN 978-1-59935-138-4
1. Tan, Amy--Juvenile literature. 2. Novelists, American--20th century--Biogra-
phy--Juvenile literature. 3. Asian American women authors--Biography--Juvenile
literature. 4. Chinese American women--Biography--Juvenile literature. I. Title. II.
Title: Amy Tan.

 PS3570.A48Z79 2010

 813'.54--dc22

 [B]

2010007594

Printed in the United States of America
First Edition

Book Cover and interior designed by:
Ed Morgan, navyblue design studio
Greensboro, NC

For Will Jacob and Elizabeth Juliana
  for the stories they've been given;
  for the stories they have yet to start;
  for the stories they will pass on

table of contents

A young Amy Tan

1

Blessings of America

"Books were my salvation."

At age fourteen, Amy Tan developed a crush on her minister's son, Robert. Tan's parents had invited Robert and his family to dinner on Christmas Eve—much to Tan's chagrin. Raw prawns, cod, tofu, and squid were on the menu, all traditional Chinese delicacies. Robert and his family were not Chinese, and when the fish was brought out, Robert squirmed. "Then my father poked his chopsticks just below the fish eye," Tan remembered, "and plucked out the soft meat. 'Amy, your favorite,' he said, offering me the tender fish cheek. I wanted to disappear."

When the meal was over, Tan's father burped loudly, which, in Chinese culture, is perfectly acceptable and is actually considered a compliment to the cook. Robert's face turned red, and his father mustered only a faint burp of appreciation. Tan was horrified.

After the guests left, Tan's mother told her:

You want be same like American girls on
the outside.

But inside, you must always be Chinese.

You must be proud you different.

You only shame is be ashame.

Years later, Tan began to write about events in her life, realizing that writing was therapeutic for her. Reflecting on the
Christmas Eve dinner and her mother's advice, she wrote, "It
wasn't until many years later—long after I had gotten over my
crush on Robert—that I was able to appreciate fully her lesson
and the true purpose behind our particular menu. For Christmas Eve that year, she had chosen all my favorite foods."

Amy Tan was given the name, *En-mai*, meaning Blessing of
America, when she was born in Oakland, California, on February 19, 1952, to first-generation Chinese immigrants. Her
father, John Yuchhan Tan, was born in 1913 in China, the
oldest of twelve children. He immigrated to the United States
in 1947. After working for the U.S. Information Service as an
electrical engineer during World War II, John became a Baptist
minister, which proved to be an important influence in Tan's
life. Her father was her mentor, and she spent her childhood
wanting to please him. Tan was fond of remembering that "his
idea of quality time with his children—since he worked seven
days a week—was to read his sermons aloud to me and see
what I thought and if there were any words I didn't understand." John found a way to reach his congregation by telling
stories in his sermons. The stories were personable and friendly.
He had a gentle way about him and was able to share life lessons with those he cared about.

Amy with her parents, John and Daisy Tan, and her
older brother Peter and younger brother John

Even though he had a good life in the United States, John
was not happy. He had fallen in love with Tan's mother, whom
he called Daisy, while he was still living in China. Unfortunately, Daisy was thrown in jail for committing adultery with
John just as he was on his way to the United States to accept a
scholarship to study at the Massachusetts Institute of Technology (MIT). He left her behind.

Over time, John Tan felt a calling to preach, partly due to
the guilt he felt for leaving Daisy in China. Unlike Daisy, John
had an absolute faith in God. He believed that through prayer
to God he could be granted "exactly what he wanted." And, it
was his prayer that Daisy be released from prison. Eventually,
she was, and she immigrated to the U.S. in 1949, shortly before Shanghai was taken over by the Communists.

Daisy's first husband had been abusive, and when she
escaped to the United States, she had to leave three young

daughters behind. Chinese law did not permit a divorced woman to maintain custody of her children. This family secret was not revealed to her American-born children until years later. Daisy kept her deep grief from the loss to herself while her children were small.

Growing up with a father entrenched in Christian faith and a mother who kept such a tragic personal history to herself was at times unsettling for Tan. Years later she would explain it like this, "Picture these two ideologies as you might the goalposts of a soccer field, faith at one end, fate at the other and me running between them trying to duck whatever dangerous missile had been launched in the air." It was common in their household to pray to God and to save a place to honor the Holy Ghost. Daisy insisted that the dinner table always included an extra set of chopsticks and a bowl for the unseen Holy Ghost.

Tan grew up listening to her mother and her aunts share stories with each other as they sat at one another's kitchen table shelling fava beans and chopping vegetables. She recalls that these women could tell stories "for hours and hours about some little detail that they found disgusting in some relative or friend."

However happy these occasions might have been, Tan admits that, more often than not, she "lived in a state of high suspense." Her mother was often depressed and had a morbid sense of looming fate. Although Tan would not learn this until years later, Daisy had witnessed her own mother's suicide when she was only nine years old. Throughout Tan's childhood, her mother's continual threat of suicide and excessive worry over someone's potential death made the house gloomy. Tan would later write:

Thanks to my mother, I was raised to have a morbid imagination. When I was a child, she often talked about death as a warning, as an unavoidable matter of fact. Little Debbie's mom down the block might say, 'Honey, look both ways before crossing the street.' My mother's version: 'You don't look, you get smash flat like sand dab.' (Sand dabs were the cheap fish we bought live in the market, distinguished in my mind by their two eyes affixed on one side of their woebegone cartoon faces.)

As a young child, Tan once talked her way out of her daily piano practice sessions her mother had insisted upon. Tan soon regretted this because her mother refused to tell her what to do after that. She made it clear it didn't matter to her any longer because she said, "Soon, maybe tomorrow, next day, I dead anyway."

Tan searched for escape from the family pressures. "Books were my salvation," she later said. "Books saved me from being miserable." Tan credits her father for being one of the reasons she liked storytelling and remembers him as a refreshing source of humor and relaxation. He read bedtime stories to his three children with great expression and did vocabulary quizzes with them from the monthly *Reader's Digest*. When she was eight, Tan won first prize among elementary school students for her essay "What the Library Means to Me." She received a transistor radio and publication of her essay in the local newspaper.

Like his children, John Tan was fearful of Daisy and was quick to give in to her demands. Foremost in these demands was that the family needed to move each time Daisy became unhappy or suspicious of their neighborhood. As a result, Tan attended eleven schools between grade school and high school graduation. She was always the new kid in school. Years later she would say that this experience was "excellent training for a budding writer." In order to learn how

Seven-year-old Amy Tan playing the piano

to fit in at each new school, she became an astute observer of other people. She was quick to learn who was popular, who was not, who was smart, and who was trouble. "It sharpened my sense of observation. It deepened my sense of alienation, which, while not a prerequisite for a writer, is certainly useful as an impetus for writing."

High school was not the only challenge Amy faced as a teenager. She was fifteen years old when her older brother, Peter, became sick and died from a brain tumor. Her father was so sure that if he prayed constantly, Peter would not die. Six months later, in 1968, Tan's father also died from a tumor. "After my father died," Tan recalled, "my mother no longer prayed to God."

Her mother was convinced that these were not random tragedies and decided their home in Santa Clara, California, harbored evil influences. Daisy began to think of where they could move next. Tan recalls that one day while her mother was cleaning house she picked up a can of Old Dutch cleanser stored underneath the kitchen sink. Her mother studied the can in her hand and then announced, "Holland is clean. We moving to Holland."

Shortly after that Daisy sold their home and bought passage for herself and her kids to Holland on the *SS Rotterdam*. Once in Holland, the family wandered from The Hague to Amsterdam and then Utrectht, because Daisy was unhappy with each location. In each city, she would search for authentic Chinese food by using sign language and odd gestures. None of them had the language skills to navigate their way through these foreign countries. It was Daisy's hope that at least the familiarity of Chinese restaurants would help the family adjust to life away from what had once been home. Over time, the family made their way slowly into Germany and then ended up in Montreux, Switzerland.

The Tan family settled into a century-old chalet in a beautiful village filled with fourteenth-century houses. This was a setting where many of the rich and famous sent their children to school. Amy's classmates were children of ambassadors, princes, and wealthy international businesspersons. She described them as "rich kids the likes of whom I had never known. One girl wore a lynx coat atop a bikini to class, much to the amusement of the young male teachers."

Tan did not feel like she fit in. Once again, Tan became the only Chinese girl in school. Angry and confused over the deaths of her brother and father, she developed an eye for noticing the small details in her life. She would notice secret pockets of sadness in others and how other people tried to hide their feelings. She didn't realize, at first, that she was developing a storyteller's skill of observing people. For each detail she noticed, she would have a dozen questions nagging her about what she was noticing. Why was this neighbor sad? Why did this friend seem bitter? Years later she would say about these struggles in her youth, "You know, those are the things that make you either psychotic or a fiction writer."

Tan realized while living in Switzerland that she was no longer "the dateless dork." She would always remember herself as the girl "who couldn't run a relay race without falling down . . . the player who sprained her finger just looking at a volleyball." She called herself the designated bungler, but when her family moved to Switzerland, everything changed.

Up till then, she said, "I was a girl who went to church every single day: Bible study, choir practice, youth sessions." In Europe, "away from the past, away from people who always thought I was this nerdy little girl, I exploded into a wild thing. I shortened my skirts, I put on makeup, I hung out with hippies. I got myself a first boyfriend, who was a German man who was 24. I was 16. And it turned out, much to my delight, that he was also the father of an illegitimate child, which made him even more despicable in my mother's eyes. . . . My mother was convinced that this man was going to ruin me."

These were hard times for mother and daughter. Tan explained that her mother had "been raised in an atmosphere of fear, that fear was the way to control children for their own good. That's what I grew up with."

At age sixteen, Tan was arrested on a minor drug possession charge. Her mother had confiscated her diary, which Tan had written in Spanish, and shared it with a detective, who had it translated into French, who used it to arrest Tan's boyfriend, Franz, and his friends. Due to Tan's age, the charges against her were dropped, but because her boyfriend was older, he was deported to Germany. This satisfied her mother, because she had been worried about Tan falling for a man who also had a history of being a mental patient and a record of having deserted the German Army.

Although she was a straight A student, it was not unusual for Tan to make such poor decisions. She felt she would never be good enough to earn anyone's high opinion of her. As a result of this low opinion of herself, she made a series of bad choices. Years later when she became a successful author, she would look back at these times and understand "kids who have made a few mistakes. They're relying on everybody else's opinion of who they are."

Although the conflict with her mother would continue for years, this particular rebellious period was the most intense. Prior to the drug arrest, Tan had threatened to run away with her boyfriend. Daisy held a cleaver to her daughter's throat, threatening to kill not only her daughter but herself and her son, John. Tan would later confess, "I was so devoid of emotion, so I just said 'Do it.' And suddenly I felt this voice—it was not me—I felt this voice come, and I heard the voice, and it said 'I want to live, I want to live, I want to live.'" This was a turning point in Tan's life. When she graduated as a junior from high school in Switzerland, Tan moved back to the United States with her mother and her younger brother, determined to move her life forward.

The San Francisco Golden Gate Bridge

2

Belief in Yourself

"If you can't change your fate, change your attitude."

In 1969, back in the United States, Amy Tan was eager to start a new life. It was time to go to college. She agreed to attend the college her mother chose and to study the courses her mother had picked out. Tan would go to Linfield, a Baptist college in McMinnville, Oregon. Her mother wanted her to pursue a degree in medicine.

Physicians made a good income and were highly regarded in both American and Chinese cultures. Tan wanted to please her mother, but it did not take long before she realized her interests and her heart were in literature. She changed her major. Tan had always liked to read. When she was small, she loved gruesome fairy tales, the grimmer the better. By age ten she had read all the Laura Ingalls Wilder books. *To Kill a Mockingbird*, by Harper Lee, which dealt with the racial segregation in the South, was also a favorite.

Reading these books made her feel grown up. Her parents

and her church were cautious about what she read, though. At one point they counseled her against reading certain books. They wanted to determine what she should believe and thought that some of the books were putting unacceptable ideas into her head. Amy rebelled against this censorship of her reading. The more she was told what books not to read, the more determined she became to read them. She would later comment:

> Reading for me was a refuge. I could escape from everything that was miserable in my life and I could be anyone I wanted to be in a story, through a character. It was almost sinful how much I liked it. That's how I felt about it. If my parents knew how much I loved it, I thought they would take it away from me.

As a result of early censure in her life, Tan remains a strong advocate for freedom of speech and warns against the danger of banning books.

Initially enthused about studying literature, Tan had a tougher time staying focused. She spent the next seven years attending five different schools. While attending Linfield College, she met Lou DeMattei on a blind date. At first she wasn't sure what to think of him, but when he transferred to San Jose City College, she followed him. Tan later said she sensed a steadiness in him that she needed in her life.

Tan transferred next to San Jose State University, where she earned a bachelor's degree in English. Later she went to graduate school and attained a master's degree in linguistics in 1974. A hard worker, Tan worked her way to these degrees on President's Scholar scholarships while also holding down two part-time jobs.

Tan warns against the dangers of banning books.

After attending both the University of California in Santa Cruz and then the University of California at Berkeley, Tan married Lou in 1974. Lou was working to become a tax attorney. Although Tan would admit years later that, while she knew him to be a good person, it took time before the two of them fell in love. One day she realized that "this is the kind of person my father was." They formed a long-lasting marriage. Tan has always been quick to give him credit for being the stable force in her life.

The newlyweds settled down in Danville, California, happy to be near enough to San Francisco to enjoy what she felt was a city of intrigue. Having grown up in surrounding cities and towns most of her life, Tan acknowledged that San Francisco had always emitted a siren's call for her. She, along with many people, had come to see San Francisco as the "city of love."

During the 1960s, musicians such as Jimi Hendrix and

Janis Joplin and other musical artists had filled the air waves. The city streets were filled with their music, funky art, and crazy clothing. Tan regarded the city as "an opera—very dramatic, historical, tragic, funny, lyrical, over-the-top."

To help pay the rent, Tan and her husband took on a roommate named Pete. Together, they shared a brand new apartment with a bull snake and a tarantula as pets. The three of them had met a few years earlier when they were all working at Round Table pizza parlor in San Jose. They would spend time after work drinking beer and solving all of the world's problems. Once Pete came to know them well enough, he confided that he had been dreaming of his death.

In exact detail, he told Lou and Tan about two strangers breaking into his room and killing him. Oddly enough, the dream didn't bother him too much because in the same dream he was able to reunite with his deceased wife. His wife had died in a car accident some years earlier, and it satisfied him that the dream ended in a reunion with her. Shortly after learning of his dream, Tan and Lou helped Pete move into his own apartment in a nearby suburb. On the night of Tan's twenty-fourth birthday, he declined their invitation to celebrate with them. They went out without him—and learned the next day that he had been murdered in his apartment while they were celebrating her birthday.

Suffering from the loss of such a good friend, Tan began to experience dreams that she would later attribute to Pete's ghost coming to visit her as she slept. There were life lessons that her good friend wanted to pass on to her, she decided. During the night, she often woke from these vivid dreams. He would talk to her and teach her lessons he hoped she would carry with her through her own life. He would tell her in these dreams,

"It's your belief in yourself that enables you to do what you wish."

At Pete's wake, Tan heard what she thought was his voice telling her the names of his attackers. "I never told the police," she said, "They would have thought I was crazy." But four days later, the two men were apprehended and their first names, Ronald and John, were the same names that had come to her through these dreams. This experience would later help her trust in the "ghostly" ways her stories would come to her. Years later, when asked if she believed in ghosts, she was careful to say, "My subconscious is open to the idea of something beyond the normal senses."

The aftermath of Pete's death was a critical time for Tan. "During this time, my life changed—or rather, I changed my life, in ways I would previously have thought inconceivable. . . . A valuable life had been lost, and to make up for it, I had to find value in mine," she later wrote. Restless with school, she abandoned her studies and began working with disabled children with speech difficulties. While working with the mentally challenged in Oakland, California, she began to understand people at a deeper level. "It was a crash course . . . about what hope means and the things that matter most."

Tan's job as a language development specialist involved working not only with children with speech problems, but also with their parents. When parents would learn that their babies were diagnosed with cerebral palsy or autism or Down's Syndrome, it was Tan's job to work with them on what to do to help the children learn to speak.

The parents would share their hopes for their children with Tan, and, then, she later wrote, "we would cry before we set

Tan described San Francisco as "an opera—very dramatic, historical, tragic, funny, lyrical, over-the-top."

out to find new hopes." She played with the kids and made them happy. Gradually she realized she was not studying the "deficits" of each child, but rather she was learning the quality of each child's soul. Tan later wrote, "From them I learned the limitlessness of hope within the limits of human beings. I learned to have compassion. It was the best training I could have had for becoming a writer." During the five years that she worked in the field, she worked with more than one thousand families.

Although she learned a great deal while working with the children and their families, Tan remained restless. She wanted to write, and she wanted to earn a good income while doing so. She left her work as a language specialist and moved into the world of freelance technical writing.

San Francisco and the surrounding area was right in the heart of the booming computer and software industry. All around were companies in need of well-written technical manuals that could be used to teach others how to use their products. Advancements in technology were happening so fast in the 1980s that manuals and technical papers were becoming obsolete almost as fast as they could be written. It was a perfect time to start up her own technical-writing business. Tan loved language and the world of words. It seemed like a good fit for her, but others didn't agree. Her mother wouldn't be happy with this career change unless Tan found a way to make more money. Tan found it easy, at first, to make a good income by doubling the hours she worked each week. Married to a man who was understanding and supportive of her decisions, Tan did not notice that her life was being consumed with work. She had no time for other activities. Worse, she was discovering that this type of writing was not satisfying.

Tan was over thirty years old and not happy in her career. Among those who discouraged her and told her she had no talent for writing was her business partner. When her partner insisted that she spend more of her time taking care of project management and leave the writing to him, she protested. Administrative duties and office work were not what she wanted to do. She argued that she should continue to write, and if she was forced to be involved in the office side of their business, she would quit and find a way to write on her own. He told her, "Writing is your weakest skill . . . You'll be lucky if you make a dime."

As a result of this conversation, Amy Tan found herself facing a hard decision. Her business as a freelance writer for the technical and business world was successful. In her industry she was well-known as a workaholic, working ninety hours a week and earning a good income. She questioned whether she dare try something different that might please her more.

Once again, she needed to find the courage to change what she was doing. To move into fiction writing, she had to find the courage to prove to her mother and others, including her business partner, that they were wrong about her ability to be a good fiction writer. Faced with the challenge, it was a time of decision that forced her to look back over her life. She began to sort through her feelings and resentments toward her mother. Tan's honest search for answers about her relationship with her mother directly led to her first success as a novelist.

The cast of *The Joy Luck Club* (1993)

3

Joy Luck Club

"Going to China was a turning point. I couldn't have written The Joy Luck Club without having been there, without having felt that spiritual sense of geography."

When Tan worked on a story, she would ask herself, "How do things happen?" She learned that she had a vivid imagination and was sensitive to small details. At first Tan tried to write stories that copied what she had read and what was already successful in books and movies. She didn't have the confidence to write about what she knew. She couldn't imagine that anyone would want to read stories about mothers and daughters fighting. Perhaps most surprising, considering her later works, is that her early characters were mostly white Americans.

The longer she wrote, though, the more she realized she needed to write for herself, and her characters should be from the culture that she had grown up in. It was good therapy to write about daughters and mothers who did not understand each other. It also made her stories better.

Gradually, her stories began to take root in the emotional center of her own life. "When I wrote these stories, it was as much a discovery to me as to any reader reading them for the first time," she told the *New York Times* in 1989. "Things would surprise me. I would sit there laughing and I would say, 'Oh, you're kidding me!'"

One of the short stories Tan wrote after quitting her technical writing business was called, "The Endgame." It is a story about an intelligent young chess player who has a hard time understanding and communicating with her China-born mother. This short story, which would later become a chapter called "Rules of the Game" in Tan's first novel, *The Joy Luck Club,* caught the interest of Sandra Dijkstra, a literary agent in Del Mar, California. Dijkstra was convinced that the literary world was ready for a novel with Chinese American mothers and daughters and asked Tan for more stories and later a proposal for a novel based on the story.

In 1986, just as her writing career began to show promise, Tan's mother was recovering from a heart attack. She was seriously ill and not showing signs of improvement. Tan was worried because her mother seemed uninterested in surviving and decided to try to bribe her with something that might bring her out of her depression. She promised her mother she would travel to China with her when she got better.

Daisy's health began to improve, and she eventually became strong enough to travel. Once her doctors approved of the journey, Tan, her husband, Lou, and her mother traveled to China in 1987 to reunite with the three daughters that Daisy had left behind decades earlier. Meeting her half sisters, now adults, for the first time was a profound experience for Tan. None of them spoke each other's language well enough to be easily understood, but all were eager to become closer.

Amy as a baby. Though born and raised in the U.S., Tan
would later come to appreciate her dual Chinese American
heritage after visiting China with her mother in 1987.

A street scene in Shanghai, China

Although Mandarin Chinese is the official language of China, there are dialects of Mandarin so different that they are essentially separate languages. Daisy Tan, however, spoke a form of Shanghainese, which is a combination of words from five different Chinese languages with an assortment of French and English words added into the mix

Shanghai had always been a city filled with immigrants from other parts of China and the world. Prior to 1949, the city was host to French- and English-speaking foreigners who

helped create this multicultural language. Daisy's Chinese daughters struggled with Daisy and Amy as each sought to communicate with each other by using an assortment of the various Chinese dialects and English.

On her first trip to China, Tan began to come to terms with her Chinese heritage. She realized how American she really was during this visit, but she also acknowledged, "It was just as my mother said: As soon as my feet touched China, I became Chinese." Coming to understand her double heritage would provide perhaps her dominant theme in her work. It also helped Tan understand and accept herself.

Having grown up in a Chinese American culture with her parents' friends and distant relatives, Tan was accustomed to many of the Chinese customs. For example, leaving food on one's plate indicates to the host that he had provided more than enough food for the guest. Should the guest accidentally eat everything on his plate as might be done in the United States to indicate that the food was good, a Chinese host would feel insulted.

Tan realized while she was in China that her mother's rules of etiquette were not mean and twisted after all. If a host were to ask his guest how long he intended to stay, the guest would realize that the host was politely letting him know it was time to leave. When the host asks the guest if he is hungry, the guest must reply that he is not hungry. If the guest were to reply that he was hungry, the host would be insulted. This way of saving face and showing respect and honor was not only important to Daisy Tan, but to Tan's half sisters as well.

While in China, Amy learned that her agent had acquired a $50,000 advance on a book that the publisher G. P. Putnam wanted her to write. This book would be based on the short story and outline of a novel that her agent had submitted.

Upon returning from China, Amy Tan was presented with the daunting task of actually writing the rest of the stories. "I wrote from nine to six and took weekends off," she said, "You have to get this done by a certain day because if you don't this chance may go away."

When it was completed, *The Joy Luck Club* told the story of four Chinese mothers raising their Chinese American daughters in the San Francisco area. *The Joy Luck Club* made the *New York Times* best seller list in 1989 and stayed on the list for nine months. It would go on to win many awards, including the Best Book for Young Adults from the American Library Association. Although Tan felt that her story spoke for all cultures and generations, the literary world considered her novel important because it offered a view of the Chinese American experience.

The novel was instrumental in paving the way for future Asian American authors because it offered a warm intimate viewpoint of the culture in a feminine voice. When asked why her novel was so tender and intimate, Tan said, "Men pan the whole scene and describe a wide panorama; their world is larger, but the sense of intimacy is not there. In my fiction and that of many women, the focus starts close-up, then the world pans out."

The Joy Luck Club is structured around a carefully assembled series of short stories. This structure allows Tan to use what is good in both short stories and novels to good effect. A short story is usually a quick, often more intimate, look into a character or group of characters' lives. It is self-standing and can be appreciated on its own. The longer form of the novel, on the other hand, is usually divided into chapters that depend on the other chapters to complete the narrative. Tan's inventive technique of weaving sixteen short stories together to form a novel was well received because each of the stories continue the narrative of several main characters in the book.

Set in California during the 1980s, *The Joy Luck Club* explores the differences between mothers and daughters, and the cultural differences between the four Chinese-born mothers and their four Americanized daughters. Tan incorporated portions of her own life and that of her mother's to portray

Between every mother and daugh

AN OLIVER STO

JOY LU

BASED UPON TH

HOLLYWOOD PICTURES presents an OLIVER STONE production a WAY
Edited by MAYSIE HOY Director of Photography AMIR MOKRI Executive Producers OLIVER STONE J
Produced by WAYNE WANG AMY TAN RONALD BASS PATRI
Distributed by BUENA VISTA INTERNATIONAL

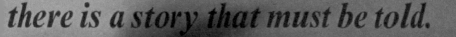

there is a story that must be told.

PRODUCTION

E

K CLUB 15

OVEL BY AMY TAN

WANG ... THE JOY LUCK CLUB" ... RACHEL PORTMAN
T YANG ... AMY TAN ... AMY TAN ... RONALD BASS
MARKEY ... WAYNE WANG   READ THE MINERVA BOOK

BUENA VISTA PICTURES DISTRIBUTION, INC.

HOLLYWOOD PICTURES

and analyze the ways in which hope and strength are passed from one generation to the next. Tan later wrote, "Certainly, the context . . . is Chinese-American. But the subtext, or the heart of the book, involves emotions we all have." Of all the characters in the book, a young woman named June becomes the main character. The story of her life loosely resembles the life of Amy Tan.

After the recent death of her mother, June is faced with the task of traveling to China to inform her stepsisters of their mother's death. Three of her mother's best friends make this journey possible. They hope that the trip will allow June, and their own daughters, to come to understand the joys and fears of their own lives.

Hope for future joy is a central theme, as it was for Tan in her own life. In the novel, the four mothers determine that, in the face of so many hardships, it is best to choose their own happiness by forming what they call a Joy Luck Club. Their daughters felt that their mothers' mah-jong-playing Joy Luck Club was an old shameful Chinese custom that didn't fit in America.

The young daughters come to realize that they had mis-understood their mothers, and that they should have pride in their Chinese heritage. This is the lesson Tan had learned in her own life. For some time, Tan did not believe in joy or luck because she had lost her father, her brother, and a best friend. Like June's experience in the novel, it took a trip to China before Tan was able to come to terms with her mother, her heritage, and, to a certain extent, the tragedies in her own life.

Although Tan did not want to earn the reputation of being an expert on mother-daughter relationships, the book focused on the ups and downs, the joys and the turmoil, between mothers and their daughters. It had always been difficult for Tan to feel adequate because her mother had had such high expectations for her daughter. For example, after the book was published with great success, Daisy told her daughter that it was too bad the book had only made fourth place on the best-seller list. She lamented that Tan should have tried to achieve the number one spot.

However painful this was for her to hear, Tan was learning to understand that her mother's criticism was the way she showed how deeply she cared for her daughter.

Another theme in *The Joy Luck Club* is that we are shaped in some ways by the stories other people tell us and by the stories we tell about ourselves. Tan acknowledged, "Any time you tell a story about yourself, it ends up being somehow fictional. . . . My brother just assumes that everything in *The Joy Luck Club* is family history. He knows it's not, but it feels like the way Mom talked."

As Tan became more honest in her writing, she came to understand why her mother lived the way she did and why she had been so strict. *The Joy Luck Club* was the beginning of a journey toward finding peace with her mother. Tan's second book, *The Kitchen God's Wife,* would continue this search for understanding and harmony between Tan and her mother.

A 1920s illustration of Tsao Chun, the Kitchen God. Tan illustrates several facets of the humble status of women in Chinese society in the early twentieth century throughout her book *The Kitchen God's Wife*.

4

The Kitchen God's Wife

"Writing is an extreme privelege but it's also a gift. It's a gift to yourself and it's a gift of giving a story to someone."

After the success of *The Joy Luck Club,* Tan wanted her mother to appreciate that the book had been written, in part, out of her growing understanding of Daisy's life. "When I was writing, it was so much for my mother and myself. I wanted her to know what I thought about China and what I thought about growing up in this country." In order to achieve this, Tan would need to be able to write her next book in a style her mother could understand. Daisy Tan spoke English as if it were directly translated from Chinese. As a result, her language was filled with imagery which Tan worked to capture in her novels.

Amy Tan stopped speaking Chinese at the age of five when she began attending schools in California. Her mother spoke with a Shanghai accent and never learned to speak English fluently. Yet, Tan felt there had to be a way that she could write this novel so that her mother would know that her daughter had come to understand her. Although some critics would suggest that Tan should not have used the "broken English" her mother spoke for characters in her book, Tan felt it was an authentic reflection of how she used language.

Her mother could read the Forbes report and study stock reports in the *New York Times* in order to make sound decisions about her stock investments. Her spoken English, however, is illustrated in an example that Tan offered in her essay, *Mother Tongue*. "One day I was saying things like 'The intersection of memory upon imagination' and the next day I would talk about the price of furniture with my mother by saying to her, 'Not waste money that way.'"

Not until later in her life would Tan spend some time seriously studying Chinese. Later, when Tan was asked to speak on a "Voice of America" radio program in Chinese, she joked, "All I could think to say was turn off the light. Don't make trouble. Go to sleep."

While Tan worked on writing in a style and language her mother could relate to, she also came to realize that she needed to understand her own mother and "what it was like to live a life of repression and to understand the fear that one has, and what you have to do to rise above that fear." Current events aided her understanding of oppression.

In 1989 Chinese students were protesting in Tiananmen Square in Beijing, China. During the 1980s Chinese students had worked on a small scale to protest corruption in the economy and the political system. One of the men instrumental in political reform, Hu Yaobang, died on April 15, 1989. At first, Beijing students gathered to set up a temporary memorial to Hu. Flowers and wreaths were placed around a photo of him. But over the next two months, events escalated to the point where thousands of students were making more and more demands of the government while at the Tiananmen Square memorial.

Martial Law was declared on May 20, 1989. This meant that instead of police enforcing the law, the People's Liberation Army (PLA) stepped in to keep the peace. These first PLA troops were peaceful and even sang songs with the student protesters, but soon the government decided to replace these Mandarin-speaking troops with a stricter division of the PLA. Unfortunately, these troops could only speak Cantonese. They could not understand what the students were shouting when they rolled their armored tanks into Tiananmen Square.

Acting under orders given by the Communist central government to clear the Square, the troops fired into the group of unarmed students on June 3, 1989. Hundreds, maybe even thousands, of peaceful citizens were killed. The rest of the world was horrified.

The death of these students was beyond comprehension for Tan, yet her mother was not surprised. Instead of taking an open stand against China's actions, Tan decided to use her writing to express the emotion and pain of the event. Daisy had grown up in China and had lived for twelve years enduring a terrible marriage under oppressive, patriarchal laws. Daisy would be Tan's muse. Responding to the Tiananmen tragedy, Tan later explained her reason for not protesting:

> What works in one country doesn't always work in another. Shaming a nation into action doesn't always work. During the time after Tiananmen Square, people thought I should go to China, stand on the square and denounce the Chinese government. . . . That would be me asserting my

View of the Forbidden City of Tiananmen Square and Chairman Mao Zedong's tomb in Beijing, China

American rights to say anything, but does it really help people who are suffering?

Inspired by the courage and bravery demonstrated by the
Tiananmen Square students, Tan decided to draw from the details of her mother's harsh life in China during and after World
War II and the Sino-Japanese War. Still, Tan faced the challenge of writing a second book as successful as her first novel.
She eventually came to realize that trying to write a story different than the first book "was an attempt at rebellion and I
realized that rebellion was not a good reason to write what I
was writing."

Daisy was eager to be interviewed and agreed to allow Tan
to videotape their long conversations. Tan learned how to ask
her mother questions, and more importantly, she learned how
to listen to the answers. The more Tan asked, the more her
mother responded. Not only was this helpful to the story line
of Tan's second book, but the relationship between mother and
daughter began to heal and grow once a mutual understanding
was allowed to develop. Daisy had the opportunity to release
the pent-up anger and fear towards her horrible life in China,
when she was married to what she referred to as a "bad man."
Tan wrote about one of the heart wrenching video sessions later
in her memoirs:

> In another memory, [Daisy] is holding a baby
> in her arms, her first son. He has just died of
> dysentery, because her husband refused to inter-
> rupt his mah jong game with the doctor. I said
> to her as gently as I could, "What did you feel
> when the baby died? You must have been in so

much pain." She looked up blankly. "No pain, only numb. I said, 'Good for you, little one, you escaped. Good for you.'"

Tan realized that as a result of a difficult childhood, her mother would naturally struggle trying to be a comforting, nurturing mother to her own children. Tan points this out by explaining that "having seen her own mother kill herself, [Daisy] didn't always know how to be the nurturing mother that we all expect we should have."

What puzzled Tan, at first, was that her mother had always calmly stated that she had not been affected by the war while living in China. Tan had to ask more questions. How could her mother not be affected? Her mother admitted that the bombs fell on her village and that she ran with the others in her village to escape the bombs when they fell. They would race to the east gate of the village when the bombs fell on the western edge of their town. Other times they would race in the opposite direction when the planes flew over the eastern side of their neighborhood. When Tan persisted in asking her mother how she wasn't affected by the war, her mother simply explained, "I wasn't killed." Tan realized then that, "my mother and I were at times oceans apart in our view of the world."

Japan had invaded China in July 1937. Within weeks, the fierce battles were being fought in the city of Shanghai—250,000 Chinese citizens died in three months. Japan was fighting under a motto known as the "Three Alls" policy, in which they were to "burn all, loot all and kill all." Surprised that China would not surrender after suffering such horrific losses, Japan marched on, determined to bring a fast end to the conflict.

Chinese paramilitary policemen present funeral wreaths during a memorial to mourn for people who were killed by invading Japanese troops during the Nanjing Massacre in Nanjing city, east China's Jiangsu province.

1937.12.13 −1938.1

In Nanjing, it is estimated that more than 300,000 civilians were killed and more than 80,000 women raped. This period of time became known to the rest of the world as The Rape of Nanjing. In China it is called the Nanjing Massacre. China pleaded with the rest of the world for help, but at this time Europe was preoccupied in trying to stop World War II, and the United States was still adamant about staying isolated from conflicts in other parts of the world. Only after the Japanese attacked Pearl Harbor on December 7, 1941, did the United States come to the aid of China by sending advisers, money, and weapons. The Sino-Japanese War continued until 1945, when the United States dropped atomic bombs on Hiroshima and Nagasaki.

Daisy's insistence that she had not been affected by this war helped Tan to understand the differences between life in the United States and life in an oppressed culture. "I decided I wanted to try to capture the shock of that difference," she realized. Exploring what can happen to a person when controlled by repressions, horrific fears, and demeaning expectations became the driving theme in Tan's second book, *The Kitchen God's Wife*, which was published in 1991.

The characters in the novel experience some of the same tragic events that her mother and other family members had suffered through. For example, Daisy's mother committed suicide at the age of thirty-nine by ingesting too much opium in order to escape living as a concubine to a rich man. In *The Kitchen God's Wife*, Winnie Louie, eventually admits to her own American daughter, Pearl, that she had been married at one time to a sadistic man and was raped by him just prior to her escape from China.

Although the details differ between the facts in Tan's family and that of the family in the second novel, the emotional truth of processing fear and oppression so that one might someday have a chance at happiness is something both families experienced. Forgiveness and hope become the difference between merely surviving tragic events in one's life and actually finding the way to embrace a deep level of happiness.

Because she wrote novels so close to her heart and based, in part, on the events in her family's life, Tan received criticism. In an interview in 2001, she admitted that the harshest criticism she had received was being accused of thinking her life is interesting enough to write about. "When people get really personal, it stings," she said.

Tan also exposed some raw truths in her novels about the relationship she had had with her mother. In writing about this relationship, Tan recalled that at the age of sixteen she told Daisy, "I hate you. I wish you were dead." Such hateful words were a result of years of angry battles between mother and daughter. The differences between generations were compounded by the differences between Daisy's Chinese upbringing and the American lifestyle her daughter fought to have. Tan was certain that she would never forget all the hurts, or be able to forgive her mother totally. Often, her mother would actually threaten to kill herself. "Okay, maybe I die, too," she would tell her daughter.

Despite these early years of tension, the power of forgiveness and love became more evident in their lives. "She couldn't have loved me more," Tan would say a few years after writing *The Kitchen God's Wife,* "there is no one else in the world who would worry for me more than my mother." Having developed a deeper respect for her mother, Tan would no longer be haunted with misgivings about their relationship. She would continue to be haunted by something, but this time she would be haunted by phantoms and ghosts.

Author Amy Tan poses in her SoHo apartment with her dog, Bubba, in 2005.

5

Sisters

"Whenever my mother talks to me, she begins the conversation as if we were already in the middle of an argument."

After publishing two best-selling novels for adults, Tan wanted to try something different. She decided to write a book for a younger audience. In 1992, her children's book, *The Moon Lady,* illustrated by Gretchen Schields, was published. A beautifully illustrated book, it tells the heart-warming story of a young girl's adventure. Her second children's book, *The Chinese Siamese Cat,* shares the tale of a cat named Sagwa. Published in 1994, and illustrated by Schields as well, the book was well received. A PBS cartoon series based on the cat was created that continued the adventures of Sagwa in a royal palace during the Qing Dynasty in China in the 1900s.

Tan's stories were attracting larger audiences of all ages. Hollywood film producers approached her with an offer to make a movie out of her first novel, *The Joy Luck Club.* Tan agreed as long she could maintain creative control. She worked with Hollywood professionals Ronald Bass and Wayne Wang to write a screenplay. Tan's experience in Hollywood was, unlike many writers, a positive one. For many writers, the stress of making a movie undermines their writing habits and practices, leaving them feeling out of the loop. Tan wrote:

> A fiction writer has the prerequisites of solitude, artistic freedom, and control. She has the luxury to go into a funk for two weeks and not get anything done. Why would any writer in her right mind ever consider making a movie instead? That's like going from being a . . . nun to serving as camp counselor for hundreds of problem children.

In addition to writing the screenplay, Tan was also coproducer and made a cameo appearance in the introductory scene of the movie. In collaboration with Wang and Bass, Tan was actively involved with and in control over the creative aspects of the movie-making process. She came out on the other end of the production drained but happy with the experience. "I can say that I went to Hollywood for many of the same reasons Dorothy found herself in Oz [as a girl who felt misunderstood]. I met a lot of remarkably nice people along the way. And they had heart and brains and courage."

In 1993, four years after first being approached about making the movie, the film was released to strong reviews. Tan would always remember watching the movie with her mother because "in striking contrast to the rest of the audience, my mother did not shed a tear. She told me after the movie ended that it was 'pretty good. In real life, everything so much sadder. So this, already much better.'"

A scene from *The Joy Luck Club*. Tan was actively involved with and in control over the creative aspects of the movie-making process.

Readers and movie-goers alike were embracing Tan's story-telling. Her style and subject matter were emotionally bonding. As an author, Tan realized how important it was to look at life and people from various angles. She was learning as a writer that each person has a point of view to be considered. On her first trip to China with her mother, for example, she learned that her half sisters had spent years feeling that perhaps they had been denied the experience of growing up with a wonder-ful, loving, and nurturing mother. However, Tan learned that her mother would get into the same arguments with people in China that she would with people in the United States. Tan had thought that perhaps the fact her mother had trouble be-ing understood in the United States frustrated her so that she was driven to argue. But even in her homeland, she continued to be difficult. Her mother would argue with anyone.

Daisy wanted to develop lasting relationships with her daughters and their families in China. She also wanted her grandchildren to learn to speak proper English. It took time

Actress Annette Benning poses between author Amy Tan and director Wayne Wang, after a screening of the motion picture *The Joy Luck Club*, in August 1993.

for them to realize she was not being overly critical. She wanted her Chinese-speaking children and grandchildren to not suffer the same pain she had to endure in the United States as a result of her poor English. Tan explained that not speaking English well in the United States meant "being misunderstood at banks, misdiagnosed by doctors and being ignored by her teenage children. Poor service, bad treatment, no respect."

There were three basic rules that Daisy constantly had tried to teach Tan: "First, if it's too easy, it's not worth pursuing. Second, you have to try harder, no matter what other people might have to do in the same situation—that's your lot in life." While Tan was willing to live by these first two rules from her mother, she was not willing to live by the third: "And if you're a woman, you're supposed to suffer in silence." Tan's refusal to remain silent had been one of the thorniest issues between them. After meeting her older half sisters in China, she found renewed strength in speaking out against this traditional attitude that kept women from finding an equal rank among men in society.

Soon after she reunited with her daughters, Daisy became the same critical mother towards them that she had been with Amy. Tan recalled that her half sisters were shocked when their mother would say, "You didn't cook this long enough" or "Why do you wear that? It makes you look terrible." As she watched her sisters work towards an understanding and acceptance of Daisy, Tan realized that she was seeing her mother from a new angle.

Tan began to understand that this was how her mother demonstrated her love and concern for her daughters. As a result of such experiences, Tan saw it was important to see things in a different light, to keep an open mind.

We all need to do that. You have to be displaced from what's comfortable and routine, and then you get to see things with fresh eyes, with new eyes. The new eyes can be very useful in breaking habits of relationships, the old irritations, the patterns of avoidance. You learn to pick what's important and say, you know, it's not so important really for me to win this one.

These were the ideas on her mind when Amy Tan set out to write her third novel, *The Hundred Secret Senses*. The novel explores the issues of love and relationships just as her first two novels had done. In this book, however, the issue of acceptance and unconditional love involves a family with peculiarities that make it difficult for two half sisters to accept each other. Kwan is from China, and Olivia, her half sister, was born in America to a Caucasian mother and a Chinese father. The sisters must learn to love each other. For Olivia, Kwan's unconditional love and acceptance is irritating. Tan had come to realize "that the kind of love that Kwan was providing was this unconditional love that felt very comforting to me, and I thought that part of me is always looking for that."

Love without expectations is a lesson Tan wanted to explore. To do so, Tan allowed Kwan, the much older sister, to have contact with ghosts. Not only did Kwan admit to having such contact, but she is able to communicate with them. This was difficult for Olivia, at six years of age, to believe at first. She struggles to understand this about Kwan, who was eighteen when she first came to the United States from Communist China. Olivia is embarrassed by her awkward half sister who believes in ghosts, and so she treats Kwan rudely. Kwan, however, continues to bestow her affection on Olivia.

Later in Olivia's life, when she is struggling in her marriage, Kwan convinces her and her husband, Simon, to travel to China with her. While the trip is designed to save the marriage, with the help of Kwan's belief in ghosts, the threesome discover they are reincarnations of nineteenth-century people caught in a struggle against Manchu soldiers in China. Kwan's coming to the aid of her sister helps Olivia get over her doubts about the "guests from another world." These "guests" had been an important part of Kwan's life, and when Olivia accepts her without conditions, she rediscovers her love for Kwan.

Tan began to realize that while she was writing about ghosts in the novel, she was perhaps beginning to listen to ghosts in her own life as well. "There are no words for it. These 'yin people' told me 'Write about us. Write about ghosts.'" This was not her first experience, however, communicating with what she referred to as "yin people." This is a term that Tan made up when trying to explain what could not be explained.

Years earlier, when her best friend, Pete, had been murdered, she had come to trust in the dreams she had after his death. In one of Pete's dream visits, he urged her to quit her job as a technical writer and explore the possibilities of writing in a way that would satisfy her more deeply. In another dream, he told her, "It's your own fears that give them [monsters] the power to chase you." She realized she could learn from the visits of ghosts once she realized that she had nothing to fear. She later wrote, "If ghosts are a delusion, then let me be deluded. Let me believe in the limitlessness of love, the beauty of contradictions, the miracle that is an ordinary part of life."

Tan further recalls that when she was writing scenes in her first book, *The Joy Luck Club,* "there were scenes in there that I thought came from my imagination, but were very strange to me." One example is a scene based on the death of

Actress Tsai Chin (right), who acted in the movie *The Joy Luck Club*, with writer Amy Tan (left).

her grandmother. Tan did not know the true circumstances of her grandmother's death, and while writing the novel, she decided to change the grandmother's status of first wife to fourth. She also had the character kill herself, which was contrary to what Tan had been raised to know about her grandmother. She had always been told her grandmother had died in a noble and yet tragic way. However, when Daisy Tan read her daughter's book she was astonished that her daughter knew that her grandmother had actually been a fourth wife—and that she had committed suicide. Amy Tan came to agree with her mother when Daisy told her, "You don't know these things, so my mother [Tan's dead grandmother] must be telling you these things."

Feeling satisfied that she had written enough about her mother in her first two books, Tan initially thought of writing a book for all her friends who had died over the years. At first the book would be "dedicated to all of my yin friends," she said. But then, after helping a close friend through a difficult illness, she made the decision to dedicate the book to her friend and editor, "Faith, because it was about having faith."

Faith Sale had been Tan's editor since 1988. Sale had coaxed Tan into writing deeper and longer stories. She was able to show Tan that what was important in her written work was what was also important in her life. A deep and satisfying friendship developed between them. When Tan's first book became a best seller she was invited to attend the American Booksellers Association convention. As both friend and editor, Sale went with her to make sure that Tan didn't let the parties "ruin her as a writer."

Tan, known for her sense of humor, felt that the most important thing Sale did for her as an editor was "keep me from embarrassing myself in public." Sale helped Tan maintain confidence in her writing as well as in her personal life. This was a friendship Tan hoped would last her entire life. But four years after *The Hundred Secret Senses* made the *New York Times* best seller's list, Faith passed away. Once again, Tan was left to find a way to move through life without yet another good friend by her side. "In Faith, I had not only an editor . . . but a mentor and a friend, someone who knew my best intentions and intuitions as a writer and how these fit in with the rest of my life," Tan later wrote.

Tan recalled that Faith would tell her grief was "finding the real heart of a story." The sadness in her life gave her the ability to tell such real, gripping stories. Tan once wrote, "But my life is excellent fodder for fiction. Memory feeds imagination, and my imagination is glutted with a Thanksgiving of nightmares." In 1995, Tan dedicated *The Hundred Secret Senses* to Faith, but she couldn't know that in four years, she would suffer even more challenges and loss.

6

Nyan-nyah

"I am like a falling star who has finally found her place next to another in the lovely constellation, where we will sparkle in the heavens forever."

Tan learned a valuable lesson when she attended a screen writing workshop at the Squaw Valley Community of Writers in northern California. She discovered that "our best stories come from our worst life experiences." This lesson would guide her writing throughout her years.

In 1999, Tan had recently completed the manuscript for a novel she would later title *The Bonesetter's Daughter* when her mother passed away from complications of Alzheimer's. Daisy had been diagnosed four years earlier, at which time Tan realized it would be important to document "the things we remember and the things that should be remembered." During the final four days of Daisy's life, Tan learned many new stories and facts about her mother's life. She had come to learn that "what I know about myself is related to what I know about her, including her secrets, or in some cases fragments of them." Daisy's diagnosis was a blow, because, Tan wrote:

> My mother had always bragged about her mem-
> ory. She never forgot anything. It wasn't that
> she remembered just dates or facts and figures.
> When she remembered an event from her past,
> especially a traumatic one, it was as though
> she had boarded a time machine and had been
> transported to the moment she was remember-
> ing. She was experiencing it again as she spoke
> of it.

Prior to finding out her mother had Alzheimer's, Tan began to notice that her mother, always a perfectionist, was leaving things unfinished. Bills were opened but not paid. Doors
were left unlocked. Daisy would forget and leave frozen food
out on the counter to rot. It was easy for some time to excuse
each simple neglect. Over time, however, her mother's tidy appearance started to decline. She would forget to bath, blaming
her shower knobs for not working. Tan would check the shower and discover that the shower was not broken. Her mother
would wear the same clothes for days on end.

The worst of these times came when Daisy was certain that
Lou, Tan's husband, had a girlfriend. Lou had always been a
loving son-in-law to Daisy. He had bought her home, took care
of her financial expenses, and was careful to serve her first at
each meal. Daisy was so sure that Lou was being unfaithful
to Tan that she took to glaring at him during their meals. She
would call Tan many times a day to tell her she had to leave
Lou. No amount of arguing with Daisy could convince her
that she was wrong.

Tan spent several weeks telling her mother what a good
man her husband was before realizing that she needed to use
another tactic. She would have to trick her mother. The next
day when Daisy called, Tan told her that she had kicked Lou
out of the house. Daisy was pleased to hear that, finally, Tan
believed her. Tan told her mom that she had finally realized

that no one cared for her as much as Daisy did. Gratified to finally be appreciated, Daisy told Tan to go get something to eat now that she had the house to herself.

But there was no food in the house, Tan told Daisy. Lou had always been the one to buy groceries, and now that Tan had kicked him out of the house, she had no food to eat. And now with Lou gone, she couldn't go out by herself to get groceries because someone might rob her. Daisy began to realize that Lou had been a good man after all. She didn't want her daughter to be alone, left in a house without any food. Perhaps, she told Tan, Lou was not a bad man, and she had been wrong about him. She told her daughter to let him stay out of the house for one night and tomorrow let him come back home. Tan thanked her mother and told her that she had saved her marriage.

Learning how to gently coax Daisy out of her wayward notions was necessary to keep her from becoming too agitated, but the day came when Tan and Lou decided that Daisy needed medical help. But Daisy was certain there was nothing wrong. They told Daisy that her blood pressure needed to be checked in order to get her to go see a doctor. Once properly diagnosed with Alzheimer's disease, Daisy was given an assortment of medication.

In addition to this diagnosis, Daisy was found to have been suffering from Major Depressive Disorder for most of her life. She was prescribed an antidepressant. Surprisingly, for the first time in Tan's life, she had a mother who was now happy and satisfied. Tan reflected, "I was saddened to think that with proper medication, my mother could have been a different person." Tan wondered if she might have "grown up to be a bubbly, well balanced, mentally stable" person had her mother been diagnosed with this disorder while Tan was still a child.

As her illness progressed, Daisy became more delusional. She often thought other people were plotting against her, and it was up to Tan to keep her calm. On the flip side of this,

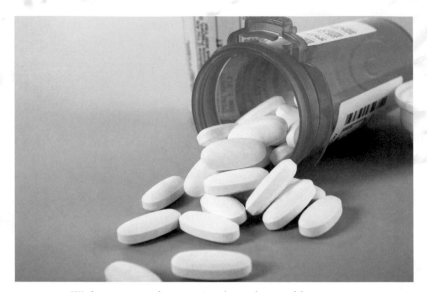

With proper medication Amy's mother could
have led a more stable, happy life.

however, her mother's defenses started to disappear. Tan could
begin to truly see her mother's loving heart, and with that
knowledge, she could easily comply in ways that made Daisy
happy. She came to realize "It had been so simple to make my
mother happy. All I had to do was say I appreciated her as my
mother."

During Daisy's final days, she began to communicate
with ghosts, calling out for "Nyan-nyah." Tan learned from
her older half sister that Nyah-nyah was a Shanghainese term
for "Grandmother." Daisy was reaching out to her own grandmother who had died decades ago.

> I remembered a story my mother had once told
> me, of her being four years old, delirious and
> near death as she called to her grandmother to
> stop the pain. My mother had been horribly
> injured when a pot of boiling soup fell across

her neck. Nyah-nyah had sat by her bedside . . . telling her that her funeral clothes had already been made but were very plain because she had not lived long enough to deserve anything more elaborate. . . . That was how Nyah-nyah, who loved my mother very much, scared her back to life. . . . This time I think Nyah-nyah was telling my mother that her funeral clothes had already been made, and not to worry, they were fancy beyond belief.

Tan would tell people later that she saw her mother's ghost. She said that twenty-four hours after her mother had passed away she "clearly saw a ghost, and she talked to me. It was my mother." Her mother's laughing face appeared to Tan, ten times larger than life. She felt physically punched in her chest as her mother's image drew closer, filling her with the sensation of "something absolute: love, but also joy and peace." Her mother told her, "Now you know, joy comes from love. Peace comes from love."

After Tan's dear friend and editor, Faith Sale, and her mother, passed away, Tan asked her publisher to give her the manuscript of *The Bonesetter's Daughter* back. "It was as though the whole essence of the book changed when they died. And I needed closure, which is why I threw myself back into writing."

Tan began to rewrite the book almost from scratch, completing it in six months. She was inspired by her own grandmother, Daisy's mother. Tan had a photograph of her and thought, "Here was a woman who is nearly unknown to everyone in the world except my mother, and she's leaving this world. She was a voiceless woman who killed herself and this legacy of voicelessness is something she passed on to my mother and, in a sense, to me." Thus began the story behind the story in *The Bonesetter's Daughter*. Tan was determined to give voice to the stories of oppressed women.

In the novel, China-born LuLing has a daughter, Ruth, who is somewhat like Tan in real life. Ruth is a technical writer and struggles with finding a good relationship with her mother. One day while attempting to clean her mother's messy home, Ruth discovers a pile of papers in her mother's handwriting. The papers tell the story of her mother's life, but they are written in Chinese characters.

Chinese writing is believed to be among the earliest written languages and is based on pictograms formed by a series of brush strokes. There are an estimated 50,000 characters. However in order to read a typical Chinese newspaper, one would need to know around 7,000 different characters.

The Chinese characters consist of two parts. One part is called the radical, which lets the reader know to which class the word belongs. The second part helps the reader know how to pronounce the word. Over time the Chinese characters have become more involved. For example, a circle with a dot in the middle once was the character for the word "sun." Now it is written like a box with a line across it. It is always possible for a good reader of the Chinese written language to come across a character never seen before.

In *The Bonesetter's Daughter*, it takes American-born Ruth time to decipher the characters used in her mother's handwriting. As the story in her mother's manuscript slowly unfolds,

Chinese calligraphy, traditional characters

Amy Tan poses for pictures at the 2003 National Book Awards Ceremony honoring Stephen King at the Marriott Marquis Hotel in New York in November 2003.

Ruth learns the truth of her mother's painful life in China and the long journey she went through to learn the truth about her own mother. In learning about her mother and grandmother, Ruth is able to determine what she wants out of life. She also discovers where she belongs.

Once again, Tan incorporates the use of the supernatural to help tell the story of Ruth's ancestors. The ghost of her grandmother talks to Ruth by helping her write messages in a sand tray with chopsticks. This leads to the discovery of oracle bones dug from caves in China. Etched into these bones are words from an ancient language. It becomes Ruth's journey to discover the story of her ancestors, a family who made precious ink and ink stones for those who practiced the art of Chinese writings, calligraphy, and bone etchings.

As was often the case in her other novels, Tan draws on the emotional truth in her life to help her write the story in *The Bonesetter's Daughter*. LuLing and her daughter, Ruth, develop a strong relationship once Ruth learns to understand the fears and joys of her mother's life. In the novel, LuLing confides in her daughter that she was worried that perhaps she had done terrible things to her and that perhaps she had hurt her daughter too much while she was growing up. It was her hope, though, as a mother, that her daughter would understand "I can't remember what I did . . . I just wanted to say that I hope you can forget, just as I've forgotten."

Through her writing, Tan is sharing with her readers what happened in the final years of her mother's life. Her mother had come to forget the bad moments in the past and reached out to her daughter for love and forgiveness. Tan did forgive her mother, and shortly after Daisy's death, she began counting Daisy as one of her faithful other-worldly muses. "I wrote of pain that reaches from the past, how it can grab you, how it can also heal itself like a broken bone. With the help of my new ghostwriters by my side, I found in memory and imagination what I had lost in grief."

7

Visions

"I write because it is about the meaning of my life."

In the summer of 2001, Tan began a forty-city tour to promote *The Bonesetter's Daughter*. Every day she was in a new city, in a different hotel, talking to new people. At times, she would wake up and look outside her hotel's window to determine what city she was in. She traveled with two small Yorkshire terrier dogs for companionship, not wanting to ask Lou to come with her. She knew how boring the tours were for him. The long hours in the hotels, airports, and stores would be difficult for anyone. She counted on the dogs to alert her to any trouble in the hotel room by barking. Anytime she could, she would sleep for twenty-four hours straight. This was not a concern at the time because she was accustomed to the exhaustion that book tours cause.

Back at home, she was in bed one night when she noticed a nude man standing in her doorway. She assumed at first it was her husband bringing her morning coffee, except it was late at night. When she called out to him, he didn't answer, so she reached out to touch the man and her hand went right through him. Tan recalled, "The only thing I could think was: 'Oh no! Lou has died and he's turned into a ghost!'" She sprang from her bed and ran through the house crying out in dismay. She ran into her living room and found her husband quietly watching TV. "Oh, thank God you're alive!" she cried. They both assumed that it was just a bad dream.

Shortly after that, though, Tan started having other visions that could not be explained. She saw a poodle dangling from the ceiling and two little girls jumping rope. One day she was certain she had watched a woman from the Victorian age working in the garden. Lou was certain that Tan's mind was becoming disorganized. Always the steady influence in his wife's life, Lou began to take on more duties around their home. Simple tasks like driving or picking up mail at the post office had become too difficult for Tan to do. Worse, she was no longer able to remember one sentence from the next when she wrote.

Lou, as always, was someone Tan could count on. Eight years earlier, he had accompanied her to the premiere of *The Joy Luck Club*. Tan was surrounded by famous people ready to watch the first screening of her movie. Annette Benning, a famous Hollywood actress, was introducing the screening when Tan realized she wanted to run out of the room. On a day that should have been one of the happiest days of her life, she was in tears and even felt suicidal.

Lou saw her through the emotional evening, keeping her steady and calm. Afterwards, he convinced her to seek medical advice. Tan agreed to see a doctor. After a careful exam, the doctor explained depression can make a person feel this way. She was prescribed with the proper antidepressants. "Like a lot of people, I had a resistance, thinking that emotional or mental problems are things that you can deal with other than through medication. I also didn't want anything to affect me mentally. But what a difference!"

Knowing how successful her treatment had been for depression, Tan and Lou were determined to find out what was causing these hallucinations. They had faith in the medical field, but two years went by before Tan could find a doctor who understood what was wrong with her. Meanwhile, she spent more than $50,000 and was seen by eleven different doctors. What was causing the joint pain, numbness, insomnia, and hallucinations? One evening while she was surfing the Internet, she came across information on Lyme disease.

She recalled two years earlier that she had pulled ticks off her dogs after hiking in the woods near Marin County, California. Lyme disease can be spread by disease-infested ticks burrowing under the skin. She had discovered a strange rash on her leg at that time. Thinking it was a blood blister, she had done nothing more than cover it with a Band-Aid for a few days.

Tan remembered that around this period of time she had "this overwhelming feeling that somebody was about to attack me. It was this constant anxiety." She didn't give it too much thought then because she had been overwhelmed at the time with caring for her ailing mother in California and her friend and editor, Faith Sale, in New York. It was easy to attribute the anxiety and joint pain Tan was experiencing to the stress of caring for her dying mother and friend.

Taking the Internet article with her, Tan was seen by Dr. Raphael Stricker, a San Francisco hematologist who had experience in treating tick-borne diseases. By this time her symptoms were advanced, and she was considered to be in the late stage of Lyme disease. To treat it, she was given three months of intravenous antibiotics.

Since the disease was not caught until it was in such an advanced stage, the doctor told her she would have severe headaches, stiffness, and numbness in her feet all her life. Further, she had to learn to accept that she must walk with a cane to keep her steady. Despite this diagnosis, Tan was relieved to discover she did not have Alzheimer's. She admitted that when she started "having memory problems and hiding mistakes that I'd made, I thought that must have been what it was like for my mother."

Even though her doctor had warned her that she would continue to have episodes and would be very sick, Tan, never one to let something keep her down, was determined to continue with her career and travels. "The terrorist in my body has been found," she later wrote. "Yes, the world to me is still a scary place, but no more so than it is for most people. I am no longer governed by fate and fear. I have hope, and, with that, a determination to change what is not right."

She formed a charity, LymeAid 4 Kids, to spread an awareness of this disease because so many doctors are hesitant to diagnose it. If it can be caught in its early stages, the prognosis for recovery is good. Most prevalent in Northern California, the Oregon Coast, the upper East Coast, and the upper Midwest, this disease effects at least 16,000 people each year.

With proper diagnosis and treatment finally at hand, Tan began to recover and wanted to get back to writing. Unfortunately, Tan continued to have a hard time with mental continuity when she wrote. She had trouble writing words in an order that made sense. In describing what it was like to write on days when her brain was suffering from inflammation, she said, "It feels like I have twelve pieces of fruit and vegetables being thrown in the air and trying to juggle them all. It's overwhelming."

Asked by her editor to consider publishing a collection of essays she'd written over the past years, Tan was hesitant. She did not like collections she considered to be "hodge-podge." If she were to do this, she would want the book of essays to have a common theme. In thinking back over the past fifteen years, she thought about what her work represented to her and realized, "It has to do with my upbringing with a father who very strongly believed in faith as a Baptist minister, and my mother, who very strongly believed in fate, and I'm trying to find things that work for me."

Lyme disease can be spread by disease-infested ticks burrowing under the skin.

With this in mind, Tan put together thirty-two chapters that explore the aspects of her life that have remained important to her. *The Opposite of Fate: A Book of Musings* was published in 2003. This collection includes the first essay Tan wrote at the age of eight, winning first prize in a contest held by the Santa Rosa Library. Tan also chose to include a funny essay about how she felt in a bookstore the day she discovered Cliff Notes were available for *The Joy Luck Club*. She wrote, "In spite of my initial shock, I admit that I am perversely honored to be in Cliffsnotes. Look at me: I'm sitting in the $4.95 bookstore bleachers along with Shakespeare, Conrad, and Joyce."

This book also includes her take on her experience as a musical performer in a group known as the Rock Bottom Remainders. Tan felt she was the last person one would expect to see in a rock 'n' roll band. She recalled that "the word 'fun' was not commonly used in our family. In our family 'fun' was a bad word." Her parents' idea of fun for the family was to take walking tours of Stanford University.

As a successful author, Tan was spending more time on the road promoting her books. Agitated and restless, Tan was in a similar situation as other authors making book tours across the nation and overseas. One day in 1991, she had received a fax asking her if she'd like to jam with a group of authors who thought it would be fun to play music together. The group wanted to perform at the next book convention in Anaheim, California, and was waiting for her reply. She thought for a few minutes and then faxed back a reply, "What should I wear?"

Within a few months, Tan was ready to sing with the all-authors group which included Dave Barry, Stephen King, Ridley Pearson, and Barbara Kingsolver. Not a skilled singer, Tan was a good sport, ready to find the fun in whatever song they were performing. The band liked to tease her about the leather costumes she wore when they played. For her own rendition of Nancy Sinatra's famous song, "These Boots Are Made for Walkin'," she wore patent-leather booties that "would transform an ordinary pair of black business pumps into awesome, man-stomping thigh-high intimidators."

In November 2002, the group was ready to perform a new song "Material Girl." Tan spent thirteen hours preparing and studying for the song but could not remember the first line. Although this memory lapse would later be discovered to be a result of Lyme disease, at the time Tan was dismayed and concerned about letting her fellow musician-authors down. The band rallied around her and helped her through the performance by having her read the words to the song on stage.

"Fun," Tan learned was found in both the joyous and dismal occasions in life. Fun was when everyone felt like family and supported one another through the good and the bad times. It was, "Hugging and being hugged by everybody in moments of sadness and triumph, because hugging is something that never came naturally to me, and now it does." Over the fun years that these author-musicians have shared with each other on the stage, The Rock Bottom Remainders have raised more than $1.7 million for a variety of literacy and book foundations striving to encourage young readers. Through the foundation, America Scores, young people are able to attend after-school programs that combine physical and social learning through creative writing. Members of the Rock Bottom Remainders meet and speak with these public school kids during their concert tours.

Books were an escape for Tan when she was young and remain a comfort in her adult years. Through the funds raised by the all-author band, it has been her hope that other children will find comfort and wisdom in books as well.

Amy Tan sings while fellow Rock Bottom Remainders member Stephen King plays the guitar during one of their benefit concerts in the 1990s.

Two Buddhist monks reading a book inside the temple in Myanmar, formerly known as Burma

8

More to Write

"Imagination is the closest thing we have to compassion."

With her health crisis under control and finally being able to read and write cohesively again, Tan was ready to write a new novel. Having made peace with her mother's memory, she was no longer compelled to center her next novel around the mother-daughter experiences.

Recalling her own journey to Burma in 2000, Tan thought to use it as the setting. The horror and tragedy prevalent in Burma, which is under the control of a military dictatorship, was not something she wanted to focus on in her story. She wanted to write a novel that could offer a sense of humor that might contrast well against the depressing atmosphere of an oppressed country.

Saving Fish From Drowning, published in 2006, is a complex novel about what happens when two diverse cultures misunderstand each other —a trademark of Tan's previous novels. This novel used the voice of a dead Chinese American art dealer to narrate. The art dealer had arranged for a tour to Burma, but dies before the trip takes place. The ghost of the art dealer accompanies the travelers and is witness to the group of Americans being kidnapped by tribesmen in Burma.

Reflective of Tan's own sense of humor, the novel balances between compassion and comedy as the tribesmen try to wrangle their own reality television show, "Junglemaniacs!," by holding the tourists hostage. Although what Tan witnessed firsthand when she was in Burma plays into this novel, while doing additional research, she discovered, "There were books out there that I never would have read about Burma. Very important books about what was going on . . . and I am left feeling 'Oh my God, I'm so sad, there's nothing I can do.'"

This novel was not met with the same success as her earlier work. Some critics felt that it was overwrought and confusing. Others, however, praised the sense of humor and felt it was a refreshing change from the mother-daughter themes in her first three books. Tan, however, had learned years earlier not to read the reviews. She knew that to stay happy and satisfied, she needed only to listen to her own inner voice. It was time to explore other areas of creativity.

In January 2006, the *Los Angeles Times* announced that they would be launching a new Sunday magazine called *West*. The new periodical would offer readers an entertaining view of the many aspects of California. With voice-driven narratives and bold photography, the magazine was highly anticipated. Tan was named the literary editor. Her responsibilities included soliciting and selecting pieces for the section "California Story." Tan was a good choice as she is a native of the Golden State and had years of success as a short story and novel writer. She was well suited for choosing original short fiction for a promising magazine of one of the most renowned newspapers in America.

Tan was enjoying the success that came from her novels. But a variety of opportunities were presented to her in other creative outlets as well. One offer came from the composer, Stewart Wallace. He and Tan had become friends years earlier when they first met at the Yaddo artist's colony. He was interested in adapting her novel, *The Bonesetter's Daughter*, into an opera. Tan initially declined to work on the project. The idea of recreating the story on stage was more than she could fathom at the time, so Wallace proceeded on the project without her.

As time went on, however, Wallace's libbrettist, or writer for an opera, was no longer able to work on the project, and he approached Tan again and told her that she could create something entirely different for the opera; she did not have to keep it based on the material in her novel. The idea intrigued Tan and she agreed to write the libretto.

To research the opera, Wallace and Tan made several trips to China. There, they traveled by ferry boat, along with Tan's half sisters, to the island of Chongming to find the very house where their grandmother lived and died. The opera was loosely based on the story of Tan's grandmother's life in China. She had lost face in her community when she was raped by a wealthy man. With no place to go, she was forced to join the man's household as one of his concubines. Eventually, she committed suicide when she realized she would have no power and no say in her life. It was believed that if one killed oneself, one could return to earth as a ghost in order to exact revenge.

Wallace, having composed five full-length operas previously, wanted to find a way to write the music so that there was a feeling of China on stage. Yet, because this would be an American opera, it was important not to alienate the American audience. Tan and Wallace agreed that it should begin in San Francisco before transporting back to China. They also both agreed that implementing the supernatural was important to

The ferry to the island of Chongming

the storyline, as was the use of Chinese acrobats, singers, and musicians in order to create a dream world to help the audience feel transported to the past.

Perhaps the most challenging part was to determine what a ghost sounds like when talking to a living person. Wallace and Tan spent considerable time debating and researching this question. In the end, Tan acknowledged, "You know, the key was really to cut out the words and let the music stand for the emotions, because that's what opera is. It's the music, it's performance, it's great voices."

Once the music and libretto were complete, rehearsals consumed Tan's time. She began to coach some of the singers, feeling that she could help them connect with the emotions of the three main female characters in the opera. In September 2008, the opera, *The Bonesetter's Daughter*, opened to a full house at the San Francisco Opera House, not that far from where Tan had been raised with dreams of becoming a pianist and physician.

Tan has always been aware that her work often told a story for someone no longer able to tell it herself. During her many travels to China, she had explored Southwest China and was entranced by a village known as Dimen. The villagers there learn to read and write in the official language of Mandarin Chinese. What interested Tan, though, was that they spoke in their own unique tongue known as Dong. Children are taught at a very early age to learn the traditional songs, which sound like cicadas chirping in the fields. Until recently, nothing had been done to document and preserve these songs for future generations.

Inspired by the people and the music, Tan wrote about her experience for *National Geographical Magazine*. In May 2008, the magazine devoted an entire issue to China. On one of her visits there, Tan had watched a young couple kiss on a bridge in Dimen. Later at dinner an older woman sang traditional Dimen songs. When Tan asked the young couple if they still sang the songs they had learned as young children, they answered that no one was interested in the old traditional songs anymore. They preferred to sing western songs in Karaoke. Tan later reflected, "So it was a very sad feeling, as I listened to this woman sing this song over dinner, that she would probably be the last person to know this song." For this reason, Tan was pleased that this music has been preserved in a collection known as *Dong Folk Songs: People and Nature in Harmony.*

Speaking up for those who cannot speak for themselves is something that has interested Tan all her life. In addition to her continued work with the America Scores literacy programs for inner-city kids, Tan's LymeAid 4 Kids foundation continues to provide funds for medical evaluation for children suspected of having Lyme disease. She serves on the board of directors of the Squaw Valley Community of Writers and has been active in the National Kidney Foundation in Northern California.

Growing up in communities near San Francisco, Tan remains in love with the Golden Gate City. Although she and her husband, Lou, divide their time between New York and California, they make their home atop a hillside in Sausalito, a waterfront community north of San Francisco, where Tan's Chinese heritage is apparent in the many scattered charms she has strategically placed throughout the house.

Although Tan says she is not superstitious, she keeps certain Chinese charms around because "Why risk displeasing the gods (or God, the Buddha, and the muses) when a subtle sprinkling of good-luck charms and a few tasteful signs of respect can make heaven smile down on earth?" Tan has three bamboo calligraphy brushes at the bottom of her computer monitor, in honor of her grandmother who Daisy believed lived in Tan's computer as her muse. Tan also has a collection of Chinese coins, mirrors with dragons carved in the frames (to swallow evil), and she practices feng shui. "What I may lack in terms of sense of style, I more than make up for by giving myself a sense of luck," Tan wrote in her memoirs. "And if my Chinese luck runs out, not to worry. I have the standard American charms as well: insurance and lawyers."

Tan's home has a panoramic view of many of the best features of the city. The park beneath the Golden Gate Bridge is world famous, but Tan prefers the nearby Presidio. This park had been a military base for more than two hundred years, first for Spain and Mexico and then for the United States. In the distance, Tan can see Alcatraz Island which was once home to the most infamous prison in the country. Looking out her living room window, Tan can see Angel Island. Although much is known about Ellis Island, the East Coast point of entry for immigrants, Angel Island is often forgotten for its role as the West Coast point of entry for immigrants. The best feature of the area, though is the Pacific Ocean. Tan would be quick to remind you not to forget the wonderful Chinese food and bookstores that have helped make San Francisco "a city with a soul."

Born and raised in a city with such soul, it is fitting that Tan has spent her years writing about spiritual journeys. Her life has been filled with turmoil and challenges and yet, each time, Tan has risen to the task of overcoming each struggle. "I think that if everything were neatly resolved, I would have no more stories to write." Tan counts on being able to write to get her through the hard times and to reminisce on the good times, and so as long as she lives, she will always have more to write about.

How is it that I am so lucky to be a writer?
Is it fate?
Is it a miracle?
Was it by choice?
Is it only my imagination?
Yes, yes, yes, yes.
It is all those things.
All things
are possible.

Author Amy Tan poses in her SoHo apartment in New York, 2005.

Timeline

1952	Born on February 19 in Oakland, California.
1967	Brother, Peter, dies.
1968	Father, John, dies; moves with mother and brother to Holland, then Switzerland.
1969	Graduates from high school; returns to United States with mother and younger brother.
1973	Earned a B. A. in linguistics and English at San Jose State University, California.
1974	Earned a M. A. in linguistics at San Jose State University, California; marries Louis M. DeMattei, a tax lawyer.
1976	Friend, Pete, dies; accepts position as specialist in language development at Alameda County Association for Mentally Retarded, Oakland, California.
1980	Accepted position as project director for MORE Project, San Francisco, California.
1983	Freelance technical writer.
1987	Meets half sisters in China, while visiting with mother, Daisy.
1989	*The Joy Luck Club* published.
1991	*The Kitchen God's Wife* published.
1992	*The Moon Lady* (for children) published.
1993	The movie, *The Joy Luck Club,* released.
1994	*The Chinese Siamese Cat* published.
1995	*The Hundred Secret Senses* published.
1999	Mother, Daisy, dies.
2001	*The Bonesetter's Daughter* published.
2003	Diagnosed with Lyme Disease; helps form a charity, LymeAid 4 Kids; *The Opposite of Fate: A Book of Musings* published.
2006	*Saving Fish from Drowning* published.
2008	San Francisco opera unveils *The Bonesetter's Daughter.*

Sources

CHAPTER ONE: BLESSINGS OF AMERICA

p. 11,	"Then my father. . ." Amy Tan, *The Opposite of Fate* (New York: G P Putnam's and Sons, 2003),126.
p. 12,	"You want be . . ." Ibid., 127.
p. 12,	"It wasn't until . . ." Ibid.
p. 12,	"his idea of quality . . ." Gretchen Giles, "Bay Area Author Amy Tan Talks about Fame and Phantoms," http://www.metroactive.com/papers/sonoma/12.14.95/tan-9550.html.
p. 13,	"exactly what he wanted . . . " Tan, *The Opposite of Fate*, 12.
p. 14,	"Picture these two . . ." Ibid., 11.
p. 14,	"for hours and hours . . ." Rita Braver, "Amy Tan, Her Mother's Daughter," *CBS News*, July 22, 2001, http://www.cbsnews.com/stories/2001/07/20/sunday/main302642.shtml.
p. 14,	"lived in a state . . ." Tan, *The Opposite of Fate*, 19.
p. 15,	"Thanks to my mother . . ." Ibid., 17.
p. 15,	"Soon, maybe tomorrow . . ." Ibid., 18.
p. 15,	"Books were my . . ." "Interview: Amy Tan Bestselling Novelist,"Academy of Achievement.
p. 16,	"excellent training for . . ." Tan, *The Opposite of Fate*, 22.
p. 16,	"It sharpened my sense . . ." Ibid., 22.
p. 16,	"After my father . . ." Ibid., 24.
p. 17,	"Holland is clean . . ." Ibid., 27.
p. 17,	"rich kids the likes . . ." Ibid., 29.
p. 18,	"You know, those . . ." Braver, "Amy Tan, Her Mother's Daughter."
p. 18,	"the dateless dork . . ." Tan, *The Opposite of Fate*, 30.
p. 18,	"who couldn't run . . ." Ibid., 129.
p. 18,	"I was a girl . . ." Academy of Achievement, "Interview: Amy Tan Bestselling Novelist."

p. 18,   "away from the past . . ." Ibid.

p. 18,   "been raised in an . . ." Ibid.

p. 19,   "kids who have made . . ." Ibid.

p. 19,   "I was so devoid . . ." Jacki Lyden, "Amy Tan:Novelist Turned Librettist" *NPR: All Things Considered*, September 13, 2008, http://www.npr.org/templates/story/story.php?storyId=94578101.

CHAPTER TWO: BELIEF IN YOURSELF

p. 21,   "If you can't . . ."Amy Tan quotes," Thinkexist.com, http://en.thinkexist.com/quotes/amy_tan.

p. 22,   "Reading for me . . ." Academy of Achievement, "Interview: Amy Tan Bestselling Novelist."

p. 23,   "this is the kind . . ." Ibid.

p. 24,   "an opera-very . . ." Cindy Loose, "Amy Tan's Guide to San Francisco," *Chicago Tribune*, March 23, 2007, http://www.chicagotribune.com/topic/am-sanfran0325,0,5099126,print,story.

p. 25,   "It's your belief . . ." Tan, *The Opposite of Fate*, 53.

p. 25,   "I never told . . ." Erica K. Caradozo, "The Spirits are with Her," *Entertainment Weekly*, October 27, 1995, 84.

p. 25,   "My subconscious is . . ." Sarah Lyall, "At Home with Amy Tan: In the Country of Spirits," *New York Times*, December 28, 1995, http://www.nytimes.com/books/01/02/18/specials/tan-home.html.

p. 25,   "During this time . . ." Tan, *The Opposite of Fate*, 52.

p. 25,   "It was a crash course . . ." George Gurley, "Interview with Amy Tan," *Knight-Ridder/Tribune News Service*, June 14, 1995.

p. 25-26   "we would cry . . ." Tan, *The Opposite of Fate*, 56.

p. 28   "deficits," Ibid., 56.

p. 28,   "From them . . ."

p. 29,   "Writing is your weakest . . ."Academy of Achievement, "Interview: Amy Tan Bestselling Novelist."

CHAPTER THREE: JOY LUCK CLUB

p. 31,   "Going to China . . ." Academy of Achievement, "Interview: Amy Tan Bestselling Novelist."

p. 31,   "How do things . . ." Tan, *The Opposite of Fate*, 36.

p. 32,   "When I wrote . . . you're kidding me." Julie Lew, "How Stories Written for Mother Became Amy Tan's Best Seller," *New York Times*, July 4, 1989, http://www.nytimes.com/books/01/02/18/specials/tan-seller.html?_r=1.

p. 35,   "It was just as . . ." *Concise Dictionary of American Literary Biography Supplement: Modern Writers 1900-1998*, (Farmington Hills: Gale Research, 1998), http://galenet.galegroup.com/servlet/BioRC.

p. 36,   "I wrote from nine . . ." Dave Mote, ed. *Contemporary Popular Writers* (St. James Press, 1997), http://galenet/galegroup.com/servlet/BioRC.

p. 37,   "Men pan the whole . . ." Ibid.

p. 40,   "Certainly, the context . . ." Tan, *The Opposite of Fate*, 190.

p. 41,   "Any time you tell . . ." Margaret Quamme, "Twenty Years of Joy," *Columbus Dispatch*, May 15, 2009, http://www.dispatch.com/live/content/life/stories.2009/05/17/2_AMY_TAN_Q_A_ART_05-17-09_E4.

CHAPTER FOUR: THE KITCHEN GOD'S WIFE

p. 43,   "Writing is an extreme . . ." "Amy Tan Quotes," Brainyquotes.com, http://www.brainyquotes.com/quotes/authors/a/amy_tan_2.html.

p. 43,   "When I was writing . . ." Lew, "How Stories Written for Mother Became Amy Tan's Best Seller."

p. 44,   "One day I was saying . . ." Tan, "Mother Tongue," http://people.virginia.edu/pmc4b/spring98/readings/Mother.html.

p. 44,   "All I could think . . ." Lyall, "At Home with Amy Tan: In the Country of Spirits."

p. 44,   "what it was like . . ." *Concise Dictionary of American Literary Biography Supplement: Modern Writers 1900-1998.*

p. 45-46,   "What works in one . . ." John Freeman, "Saving Fish From Drowning: Amy Tan," *Sacramento News and Record*, November 24, 2005, http://www.newsreview.com/sacramento/content?oid=44749.

p. 48,   "was an attempt at . . ." Mervyn Rothstein, "A New Novel by Amy Tan, Who's Still Trying to Adapt to Success," *New York Times*, June 11, 1991, http://www.nytimes.com/books/01/02/18/specials/tan-adapt.html.

p. 48-49,   "In another memory . . ." Tan, *The Opposite of Fate*, 82.

p. 49,   "having seen her own . . ." Academy of Achievement, "Interview: Amy Tan Bestselling Novelist."

p. 49,   "I wasn't killed . . ." Tan, *The Opposite of Fate*, 208.

p. 49,   "my mother and I . . ." Ibid., 208.

p. 51,   "I decided I wanted . . ." Rothstein, "A New Novel by Amy Tan, Who's Still Trying to Adapt to Success."

p. 52,   "When people get really . . ." Laurel Narersen, "Write guard: Bizarre Asks Five Fiction Masters About the Agony and Acstasty of Modern Literary Life," *Harper's Bazaar*, June 2001, 117.

p. 52,   "I hate you . . ." Marlo Thomas, *The Right Words at the Right Times* (New York: Atria Books, 2002), 339.

p. 52,   "Okay, maybe I die . . ." Ibid.

p. 52,   "She couldn't have loved . . . " Braver, "Amy Tan: Her Mother's Daughter."

CHAPTER FIVE: SISTERS

p. 55,   "Whenever my mother . . ." "Amy Tan quotes," Thinkexist.com, http://en.thinkexist.com/quotes/amy_tan.

p. 56,   "A fiction writer . . ." Tan, *The Opposite of Fate*, 178.

p. 56,   "I can say that . . ." Ibid., 178.

p. 56,   "in striking contrast to . . ." Tan, *The Opposite of Fate*, 202.

p. 60,   "being misunderstood at banks . . ." Ibid., 165.

p. 60,   "First if . . . " *Concise Dictionary of American Literary Biography Supplement: Modern Writers 1900-1998.*

p. 60,   "You didn't cook . . ." Academy of Achievement, "Interview: Amy Tan Bestselling Novelist."

p. 61,   "We all need to . . ." Ibid.

p. 61,   "that the kind of . . . " Quamme, "Twenty Years of Joy."

p. 62,   "There are no words . . ." Caradozo, "The Spirits are with Her," 84.

p. 62,   "It's your own fears . . ." Tan, *The Opposite of Fate,* 53.

p. 62,   "If ghosts are a delusion . . ." Ibid., 266.

p. 62,   "there were scenes in . . ." Quamme, "Twenty Years of Joy."

p. 64,   "You don't know these things . . ." Ibid.

p. 64,   "dedicated to all of . . . " Gretchen Giles, "Bay Area Author Amy Tan Talks About Fame and Phantoms," *Sonoma Independent,* December 14, 1995, http://www.metroactive.com/papers/sonoma/12.14.95/tan-9550.html.

p. 64,   "ruin her as a . . ." Tan, *The Opposite of Fate,* 61.

p. 64-65,   "keep me from . . ." Ibid., 63.

p. 65,   "In Faith, I had . . ." Ibid.

p. 65,   "finding the real heart . . ." Ibid., 96.

p. 65,   "But my life . . ." Ibid., 33.

CHAPTER SIX: NYAN-NYAH

p. 67,   "I am a falling star . . ." "Amy Tan quotes," Thinkexist.com, http://en.thinkexist.com/quotes/amy_tan.

p. 67,   "our best stories come . . ." Tan, *The Opposite of Fate,* 179.

p. 67,   "the things we remember . . ." Paul Gray, and Andrea Sachs, "The Joys and Sorrows of Amy Tan," *Time,* February 19, 2001, http://www.time/com/time/printout/0,8816,999251,00.html.

p. 67,   "what I know about . . ." Tan, *The Opposite of Fate,* 74.

p. 68,   "My mother had always . . ." Ibid, 81.

p. 69,   "I was saddened to think . . ." Ibid., 90.

p. 69,   "grown up to be . . ." Ibid.

p. 70-71, "It had been so simple . . ." Ibid., 93.

p. 71,   "I remembered a story . . ." Ibid., 95.

p. 71,   "clearly saw a ghost . . ." Jay Allison, Dan Gediman, John Gregory, and Viki Merrick, "Saying Thanks to My Ghosts," *Weekend Edition Sunday*, April 26, 2009.

p. 71,   "It was as though . . ." Jane Ganahl, "Amy Tan Gets Her Voice Back," *Book*, January, 2001, 40.

p. 71,   "Here was a woman who . . ." Braver, "Amy Tan: Her Mother's Daughter."

p. 75,   "I can't remember what . . ." Gray, "The Joys and Sorrows of Amy Tan."

p. 75,   "I wrote of pain . . ." Tan, The Opposite of Faith, 97.

CHAPTER SEVEN: VISIONS

p. 77,   "I write because . . ." Academy of Achievement, "Interview: Amy Tan Bestselling Novelist."

p. 78,   "The only thing I . . ." Michelle Tauber, "A New Ending," *People Weekly*, November 3, 2003.

p. 78,   "Oh, thank God you're . . ." J. J. McCoy, "Amy Tan, Ticked Off About Lyme," *Washington Post*, August 5, 2003, http://www.canlyme.com/amy.html.

p. 78,   "Like a lot of people . . ." Andrea Sachs, "The Joys and Sorrows of Amy Tan," *Time*, Feb 2001, 72.

p. 79,   "this overwhelming feeling that . . ." Tauber, "A New Ending."

p. 79-80, "having memory problems and . . ." McCoy, "Amy Tan, Ticked Off About Lyme."

p. 80,   "The terrorist in my body . . ." Tan, *The Opposite of Fate*, 398.

p. 80,   "It feels like I . . ." Jay MacDonald, "A Date with Fate," *Book Page*, November 2003, http://www.bookpage.com/0311bp/amy_tan.html.

p. 80,   "It has to do with . . ." Ibid.

p. 81,	"In spite of . . ." Tan, *The Opposite of Fate*, 10.
p. 81,	"the word 'fun' was . . ." Ibid., 136.
p. 82,	"What should I wear . . ." Ibid., 139.
p. 82,	"would transform an . . ." Ibid, 146.
p. 82,	"Hugging and being hugged . . ." Ibid, 153.

CHAPTER EIGHT: MORE TO WRITE

p. 87,	"Imagination is the . . ." Amy Tan, "A Conversation with Amy Tan by Lawrence Bridges," http://www.daylife.com/topic/Amy_Tan.
p. 88,	"There were books out . . ."Malcolm Jones, "A Lighter Look at Suffering," *Newsweek*, October 24, 2005, 16.
p. 92,	"You know, the key . . ." Lyden, "Amy Tan: Novelist Turned Librettist."
p. 93,	"So it was a very . . ." "Amy Tan Reveals Stories of Dong Folk Songs," *NPR: All Things Considered*, April 25, 2008, http://www.npr.org.templates/story/story.php?storyId=89943080.
p. 93,	"Why risk displeasing . . ." Tan, *The Opposite of Fate*, 231.
p. 94,	"What I may lack . . ." Ibid., 234.
p. 94,	"a city with a soul . . ." Loose, "Amy Tan's Guide to San Francisco."
p. 94,	"I think that if . . ." Lew, "How Stories Written for Mother Became Amy Tan's Best Seller."
p. 95,	"How is it . . ." Tan, *The Opposite of Fate*, 38.

Bibliography

Aero, Rita. *Things Chinese*. Garden City, New York: Doubleday, 1980.

Allison, Jay, Dan Gediman, John Gregory, and Viki Merrick. "Saying Thanks to My Ghosts." *Weekend Edition Sunday*, April 26, 2009.

Boli, Zhang. *Escape from China, The Long Journey from Tianamen to Freedom*. New York: Washington Square Press, 2003.

Braver, Rita. "Amy Tan: Her Mother's Daughter." *CBS News*, July 22, 2001. http://www.cbsnews.com/stories/2001/07/20/sunday/main302642.shtml.

Caradozo, Erica K. "The Spirits Are with Her." *Entertainment Weekly*, October 27, 1995.

Chai, May-lee, and Winberg Chai. *China A to Z Everything You Need to Know to Understand Chinese Customs and Culture*. London: Penguin Books, 2007.

————. *Concise Dictionary of American Literary Biography Supplement: Modern Writers 1900-1998*. Farmington Hills: Gale Research, 1998, http://galenet.galegroup.com/servlet/BioRC.

Dee, Johnathan. *Simply Chinese Astrology*. New York: Sterling Publishing, 2006.

Dramer, Kim. *People's Republic of China Enchantment of the World*. New York: Children's Press, 2007.

Ferroa, Peggy Grace. *Cultures of the World: China*. New York: Marshall Cavendish, 2002.

Flower, Kathy. *China: A Quick Guide to Customs and Etiquette*. Portland: Graphics Arts Center Publishing, 2003.

Freeman, John. "Saving Fish From Drowning: Amy Tan." *Sacramento News and Record*, November 24, 2005. http://www.newsreview.com/sacramento/content?oid=44749.

Ganahl, Jane. "Amy Tan Gets Her Voice Back." *Book*, January 2001.

Giles, Gretchen. "Bay Area Author Amy Tan Talks about Fame and Phantoms." *Sonoma Independent*, December 14, 1995. http://www.metroactive.com/papers/sonoma/12.14.95/tan-9550.html.

Gray, Paul, and Andrea Sachs. "The Joys and Sorrows of Amy Tan." *Time*, February 19, 2001. http://www.time/com/time/printout/0,8816,999251,00.html.

Gurley, George. "Interview with Amy Tan." *Knight-Ridder/Tribune News Service*, June 14, 1995.

Jones, Malcolm. "A Lighter Look at Suffering." *Newsweek*, October 24, 2005.

Lew, Julie. "How Stories Written for Mother Became Amy Tan's Best Seller." *New York Times*, July 4, 1989. http://www.nytimes. com/books/01/02/18/specials/tan-seller.html?_r=1.

Loose, Cindy. "Amy Tan's Guide to San Francisco." *Chicago Tribune*, March 23, 2007. http://www.chicagotribune.com/topic/am-sanfran0 325,0,5099126,print,story.

Lyall, Sarah. "At Home With Amy Tan: In the Country of Spirits." *New York Times*, December 28, 1995. http://www.nytimes.com/ books/01/02/18/specials/tan-home.html.

Lyden, Jacki. "Amy Tan Novelist Turned Librettist." *NPR: All Things Considered*, September 13, 2008. http://www.npr.org/templates/ story/story.php?storyId=94578101.

MacDonald, Jay. "A Date with Fate." *Book Page*, November 2003. http://www.bookpage.com/0311bp/amy_tan.html.

Major, John S. *The Land and People of China*. New York: J B Lippincott, 1989.

McCoy, J. J. "Amy Tan, Ticked Off About Lyme." *Washington Post*, August 5, 2003. http://www.canlyme.com/amy.html.

Michaels, Spencer. "Amy Tan, San Francisco Opera Takes Novel From Page to Stage." *PBS Newshour*, September 25, 2008.

Mote, Dave, ed. *Contemporary Popular Writers*. Farmington Hills: St. James Press, 1997. http://galenet/galegroup.com/servlet/BioRC.

Narersen, Laurel. "Write Guard: Bazaar Asks Five Fiction Masters About the Agony and Acstasy of Modern Literary Life." *Harper's Bazaar*, June 2001.

Pearl, Nancy. "Amy's Legacy: Asian American Fiction." *Library Journal*, September 15, 2000.

Quamme, Margaret. "Twenty Years of Joy." *Columbus Dispatch*, May 15, 2009. http://www.dispatch.com/live/content/life/ stories.2009/05/17/2_AMY_TAN_Q_A_ART_05-17-09_E4 .

Rothstein, Mervyn. "A New Novel by Amy Tan, Who's Still Trying to Adapt to Success." *New York Times*, June 11, 1991. http://www.nytimes.com/books/01/02/18/specials/tan-adapt.html.

Sachs, Andrea."The Joys and Sorrows of Amy Tan." *Time*, Feb 2001.

Tan, Amy. "Mother Tongue." http://people.virginia.edu/pmc4b/spring98/readings/Mother.html.

———. *The Opposite of Fate*. New York: G P Putnam's and Sons, 2003.

Tauber, Michelle. "A New Ending." *People Weekly*, November 3, 2003.

Thomas, Marlo. *The Right Words at the Right Times*. New York: Atria Books, 2002.

Willard, Nancy. "Talking to Ghosts." *New York Times*, February 18, 2001. http://www.nytimes.com/books/01/02/18/010218.18williat.html.

———. "Amy Tan Reveals Stories of Dong Folk Songs." *NPR: All Things Considered*, April 25, 2008. http://www.npr.org.templates/story/story.php?storyId=89943080.

———. "Best Selling Authors Kick Off Their First West Coast 'Fire in the Belly' Tour." *PRNewswire*, February 27, 2008.

———. "Los Angeles Times to Launch 'West' Magazine." *PRNewswire*, January 12, 2006.

———. "The Spirit Within." *The Salon Interview*, November 12, 1995. http://www.salon.com/12nov1995/feature/tan/html.

———. "Amy Tan Takes Over." *Book Page*, September 2008.

Web Sites

http://www.achievement.org/autodoc/printmember/tan0int-1.
Academy of Achievement.
  "Interview: Amy Tan Best-Selling Novelist."

http://www.princetonlibrary.org.
Princeton Library. "Amy Tan."

http://www.amytan.net
Amy Tan's personal Web site

Index

Picture Credits

8:      Courtesy of Amy Tan. Reprinted by permission of the author and the Sandra Dijkstra Literary Agency

10:      Courtesy of Amy Tan. Reprinted by permission of the author and the Sandra Dijkstra Literary Agency

13:      Courtesy of Amy Tan. Reprinted by permission of the author and the Sandra Dijkstra Literary Agency

16:      Courtesy of Amy Tan. Reprinted by permission of the author and the Sandra Dijkstra Literary Agency

20:      Used under license from iStockphoto.com

23:      Used under license from iStockphoto.com

26-27:   Used under license from iStockphoto.com

30-31:   Moviestore collection Ltd/Alamy

33:      Courtesy of Amy Tan. Reprinted by permission of the author and the Sandra Dijkstra Literary Agency

34-35:   Used under license from iStockphoto.com

38-39:   Moviestore collection Ltd/Alamy

42:      Lordprice Collection/Alamy

46-47:   Used under license from iStockphoto.com

50:      Imaginechina via AP Images

54:      AP Photo/Joe Tabacca

57:      United Archives GmbH/Alamy

58-59:   Associated Press

63:      Trinity Mirror/Mirropix/Alamy

66:      Used under license from iStockphoto.com

70:      Used under license from iStockphoto.com

72-73:   LOOK Die Bildagentur der Fotografen GmbH/Alamy

74:      LAURA CAVANAUGH/UPI /Landov

76-77:   Used under license from iStockphoto.com

81:      Used under license from iStockphoto.com

84-85:   Associated Press

86-87   Used under license from iStockphoto.com

90-91:   Associated Press

96-97:   AP Photo/Joe Tabacca